Winchester Public Library
Winchester, MA 01890
781-721-7171
www.winpublib.org

SandCastle™

Farm Pets

Gleeful Goats

Colleen Dolphin
AUTHOR

C.A. Nobens
ILLUSTRATOR

Consulting Editor, Diane Craig, M.A./Reading Specialist

ABDO
Publishing Company

Published by ABDO Publishing Company, 8000 West 78th Street, Edina, Minnesota 55439.

Copyright © 2011 by Abdo Consulting Group, Inc. International copyrights reserved in all countries.

Printed in the United States of America, North Mankato, Minnesota
052010
092010

 PRINTED ON RECYCLED PAPER

Editor: Liz Salzmann
Content Developer: Nancy Tuminelly
Cover and Interior Design and Production: Colleen Dolphin, Mighty Media
Photo Credits: Shutterstock

Library of Congress Cataloging-in-Publication Data
Dolphin, Colleen, 1979-
  Gleeful goats / Colleen Dolphin.
    p. cm. -- (Farm pets)
  ISBN 978-1-61613-371-9
  1. Goats--Juvenile literature. I. Title.
SF383.35.D65 2010
636.3'9--dc22
                        2009053102

SandCastle™ Level: Transitional

SandCastle™ books are created by a team of professional educators, reading specialists, and content developers around five essential components—phonemic awareness, phonics, vocabulary, text comprehension, and fluency—to assist young readers as they develop reading skills and strategies and increase their general knowledge. All books are written, reviewed, and leveled for guided reading, early reading intervention, and Accelerated Reader® programs for use in shared, guided, and independent reading and writing activities to support a balanced approach to literacy instruction. The SandCastle™ series has four levels that correspond to early literacy development. The levels are provided to help teachers and parents select appropriate books for young readers.

Emerging Readers	Beginning Readers	Transitional Readers	Fluent Readers
(no flags)	(1 flag)	(2 flags)	(3 flags)

SandCastle™ would like to hear from you. Please send us your comments and suggestions.
sandcastle@abdopublishing.com

Contents

Goats

Goats are very friendly animals. They like a lot of attention. They can be very fun pets!

Billy gives his goats food and fresh water each day. He feeds them hay.

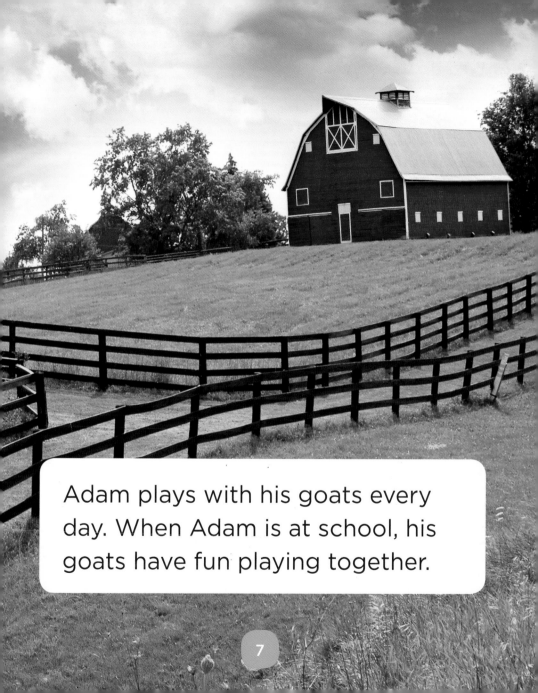

Adam plays with his goats every day. When Adam is at school, his goats have fun playing together.

Sarah's goats have a large field to **explore**. They like to munch on **brush** and grass.

Goats like to stay dry. They find **shelter** when it rains.

Sam has a large rock to climb on. Climbing on rocks helps **groom** his hooves.

A Goat Story

Denny and his brother
Jim went for a walk.
They spotted a goat
that was eating a sock!

Jim looked at its tag and said, "You're a long way from home!" Denny said, "Yes, Lucky the goat must like to **roam**."

The boys wanted
to take Lucky back.
So they led him along
with a trail of snacks.

They walked through
fields to the Olsen farm.
Farmer Olsen was glad
to see his Lucky **charm**!

Did You Know?

* A goat that is younger than six months is called a *kid*.

* Most goats live for 10 to 12 years. Some goats live up to 30 years!

* Goats are very good at climbing.

* A group of goats is called a *trip*.

* Goats are very good swimmers.

Goat Quiz

Read each sentence below. Then decide whether it is true or false!

1. Goats do not like attention.

2. Goats like to eat grass.

3. When it rains, goats find **shelter**.

4. Denny and Jim find a goat eating a shoe.

5. Farmer Olsen is glad to see Lucky.

Glossary

brush – an area where bushes and short trees grow.

charm – something that is believed to bring good luck.

explore – to learn about a place by walking all around it.

groom – to take care of an animal's fur, nails, claws, or hooves.

roam – to go from place to place.

shelter – protection from the weather.

To see a complete list of SandCastle™ books and other nonfiction titles from ABDO Publishing Company, visit www.abdopublishing.com.

8000 West 78th Street, Edina, MN 55439 • 800-800-1312 • fax 952-831-1632